Step into Change:

Crafting your Career in Change Management

By Naomi Jones-Black

With foreword by Helen Campbell,

co-founder of the Change Management Institute

© CMO-1 2024 (ISBN: 979-8-32-922869-4)

Disclaimer: This book is an opinion piece. Change management roles can earn $200+. This book is not intended to provide advice that can be relied upon to result in financial gain.

About the Author

Naomi Jones-Black is the Principal Advisor of CMO-1, an organisational change management advisory service based in Hobart, Tasmania, Australia. She started her change management career in 2007. Naomi holds a Master of Business, Graduate Diploma in Management and a Bachelor of Commerce. She is a Change Management Practitioner and an Accredited Change Management Professional.

Naomi skilfully creates, curates and distributes content to build change capability for people and organisations to be excellent change makers. She believes in the power of collaboration and is passionate and keen to impart her knowledge and experience in organisational change management. She desires for organisations to become better at designing, implementing, and managing change. She is the author and editor of *'The Power of People Collaborating: Change management perspectives'*.

Naomi is a people manager with many years experience and as a Head of Change, has led change teams and held responsibility for enterprise-wide change frameworks. She is accredited in the Human

Synergistic organisational culture tools, Lifestyle Inventory and Group Styles Inventory.

She has worked in many functions in business including procurement, finance, HR, risk management, information management and project management. Sectors Naomi has worked in include telecommunications, the electricity supply industry, professional performing arts management, marine resources, justice and corrections and emergency services.

In 2023, Naomi joined the global Board of the Change Management Institute, a global, independent, not-for-profit organisation set up to promote and develop the profession of change management internationally.

Table of Contents

Foreword 1

Preface 3

Introduction 6

Chapter 1. Why be a Change Professional when you Grow Up? 12

Chapter 2. Your Career Path Towards Change 16

Chapter 3. Have You Qualified? 26

Chapter 4. Do You Naturally Have What It Takes? 30

Chapter 5: So, what about Change Leadership? 35

Chapter 6. A Week in the Life of a Change Professional 39

Chapter 7: The Darker Sides of Change Management 44

Chapter 8. Do You Have the Character? 50

Chapter 9. Your Steps Towards Change 54

Chapter 10. Pre-decide your principles 61

Chapter 11. Put it Altogether 67

Foreword

When Naomi asked me to write a forward for her book, I was both humbled and excited. I've been a part of the change management profession for over 30 years and the most common question I'm asked is: "How do I get into change management?" The answer can be complicated so Naomi has poured all the practical advice you'll ever need into this book. She's an insider who's been there. Rarely do you get access to pearls of wisdom like this in one place.

Change Management has been a recognised profession for over 20 years and the disciplines that underpin it have been around much longer. The professional infrastructure (frameworks, models and standards) has matured during that time. You'll be joining a profession that is still young enough to be fresh and open but mature enough to provide the structure you'll need to grow in the role. Change Management can sometimes feel less defined compared to related professions but don't let that put you off. Change Management looks different in different organisations. Change professionals are chameleons. We operate at different levels and in different environments; often flexing to provide whatever support is required at that time and place (always grounded in a solid body of knowledge and our trusty toolkit). It's this variety that enables people from diverse backgrounds to find a change role that suits them.

Change professionals come from all walks of life. The broad nature of the role provides a rare opportunity to incorporate knowledge, skills and experience from whatever career or study path has come before. As Naomi points out, a genuine interest in helping people navigate through periods of uncertainty and disruption is the main prerequisite. It's this that gives the Change Manager the satisfaction of knowing they're making a difference through their work.

It's almost a cliché nowadays to say that 'change is the only constant'. (Hasn't that always been the case?) But there's no doubt that the volume, pace and complexity of change continues to take our organisations and their people into unchartered waters. The world needs more great change professionals to help them navigate those waters.

As you move through the sound advice contained in this book, you will uncover the path towards the most meaningful, exciting and challenging career in today's organisations. We'd love to have you in the change management family.

Helen Campbell

June 2024

Preface

I was snowboarding in France, working a winter job with a UK company, when I reconnected with a past love, who within three months, flew to Rome to meet me and within three days, asked for my hand in marriage. We married and I moved countries, again.

Before my 9-month snowboarding stint in the French Haute-Savoie mountains, I was experienced in project management. I was trained in business – banking and finance to be exact. For 3 years in London, I was in my first management job, while I completed my Master of Business. When the 2005 London bombings hit Tavistock Square, around the corner from my workplace, I was on a rare work-from-home day. I was happily going about my morning when my parents called me from Australia to ask if I was OK. Huh, why? Naomi, turn on the news, they said.

The days and weeks following the London bombings, I found it to be deeply unsettling. The Tube was not running, so I turned to the local bus service. Buses, heaving with passengers, went past me one after the other without stopping. I borrowed a bike from my flatmate, determined to get to my office, no matter how long it took. I couldn't face riding on the road, the hectic traffic looked like a death trap to me. On my first ride, I was stopped by a police officer who told me that it was illegal to ride on the footpath. I burst into tears. It was at that moment that I decided to leave London and go snowboarding in France.

My upbringing was gypsy-like. My father was in the Royal Australian Air Force, so our family moved around a lot. I was used to moving and kept going as an adult. My soon-to-be husband and I had met in a country town in New South Wales and went to high school together but he moved to Hobart Town, while I was overseas for almost 5 years. I arrived in Hobart with a backpack and not much else to my name. I got onto my first task: get a job. Moving to Hobart meant that I gave up my previous career, where I was already at management level. But there were absolutely no jobs in my field on the regional island.

It was the price of love. I took what I could get and joined a temping agency. There I was, a newly qualified Master of Business, hole punching for Zeehan Zinc Pty Ltd. But you've got to do what you've got to do, right? We had a wedding to pay for. My employment agency called me one day to ask if I could pop down to a place called Aurora Energy for a chat. I thought it'd be another a hole-punching gig. When I got there, it was a job interview with a panel of two, for a role called Change Manager. I had never heard of it! They asked me questions and I answered honestly. They saw that I was cluey and could probably work it out, so they hired me for a 3-month gig. That was in 2007 and I am still in the role. I've swapped organisations and industries a few times but I'm still a "Change Manager". It's the best job in the world.

Introduction

This is the book that I wish I had when I first transitioned into becoming a change professional. You too must be interested in the role, which is why you opened this book. Right now, you might be from another business discipline, as I was, or you are a student and looking for advice on options for your future. Or you are looking for more personal fulfilment out of your j-o-b. This book is essentially about employment in a satisfying purpose-driven career.

This book is equally useful for people, right now, who are in complementary fields to change management such as human resources, organisational development, training, and even project managers, business analysts and risk managers. If so, your current role has developed specific competencies in you that are immediately applicable to change management.

It is also for individual consultants who may want to add change management to their offerings. While we will focus on the role of change professional working within an organisation, by the same token, this book is about the role of Change Consultant. By my definition (specialisation aside) a Change Consultant does the same job as an in-house Change Manager.

What this book covers:

1. Why anyone would want to be a change professional when they grow up.
2. Why there is a shortage of change professionals and where the future demand is going to be.
3. What essential qualifications and character traits change professionals need.
4. A week in the life of a change professional, with some practical insights into what the job involves on a day-to-day basis.
5. A warning about the darker side of change management, so that you can go into this career with eyes wide open.

Then, if you are still with me amongst all the home truths and challenges, we finish up with some practical ideas and career hacks so you are ready to craft your career in change management.

This book promises to help you become a change professional. Better still, reading this should inspire you to be an excellent change person. Excellence is the bar. Because if we are excellent, our organisations can be excellent. And if organisations can be excellent, so too can the business world be.

I intend to make this a quick read because I know you are a busy person. There's an inevitable trade-off between a quick read and a comprehensive read. This is quick. That means there will be some details left out and skipped over. Of course, there is more to the story as we transition rapidly from chapter to chapter, and from topic to topic but this should be enough to get you inspired and get you started in a useful direction.

Why the world needs more Change Professionals

So that we are clear on the context for this book when I say 'change management' what I mean is the planned set of activities designed to ensure that stakeholders utilise the outputs delivered by organisations, in order to realise the intended benefits. To this day, people still don't understand what change management is. A colleague described it to me as being like the Olympic sport of curling. The objective of curling is to slide a heavy rock over ice to end up as close to the target as possible. How the rock slides can be influenced by two people who 'sweep' the ice in order to help reduce the friction for the rock. The rock is the objective of the change, the sweepers are the change professionals.

In this book, I will use the term "change professional" to mean any kind of role working on the people side of change. The term "Change Manager" is becoming out of fashion, because the change guild generally feel that the "manager" word denotes a person working at a certain level in an organisation. When I reached out to colleagues to help me with a title for this book, one, rightly, pointed out that change practitioners are also Directors, Leaders, Heads of Change or Vice Presidents with so much more influence than managers! There is now even a path from change to the C-suite. Although I still do refer to a "Change Manager" role at times, largely when I talk about a change professional in this book, I mean all of those possible roles of which "Change Manager" is one possibility.

In the widest possible context, change management is essential for all organisations. Between sustainability targets for climate change and the bow-wave of disruption that Artificial Intelligence (AI) will hand us, the case for change management is already firmly established. We know that constant change is the new normal for organisations.

It is generally thought that the jobs of the future, which will be immune to takeover by AI, will require a high degree of human interaction and competence in social and emotional intelligence. Change management is one of those jobs. Nobody wants a "Computer says "No!" situation when you are dealing with people's lives. Automation of change management is already here, with increasing investment in software to manage the swathes of change data. But taking action on the data, creating strategy, and truly understanding the complex social sphere, is wholly human because it involves the interpretation of the intelligence that has been gathered, about people's motivations, life situations, experiences of the past, and attitudes. Every change is different and nuanced. Every change involves a different set of humans. I'll state this now and you can fact-check me in 20 years: No AI can truly understand human behaviour in organisations. Nor should we give it the power to try.

So, the role of the change professional is here to stay. In fact, the widespread implementation of AI will quickly become a growth field for change professionals. There is a case for change to be defined, a vision to be articulated, and a future state to be described and reached. Case by case, each change professional will need to resolve within themselves where they stand on the ethics of implementing AI in different contexts and in different countries. AI is coming and it's going to need change professionals to help people to adapt.

Another growth area for change professionals is the increasing focus on Environmental, Sustainability, and Governance. ESG targets have meant that organisations must transform business operations to meet community, and even, activist expectations. It's not just reporting on ESG that is the change. It is the underlying practices and business processes where the true change lies. For example, where organisations commit to a B-Corp Certification, they need good change professionals to help with the change. B-Corp

Certification measures a company's social and environmental impact across the whole organisation and is a mark of excellence.

The conversation will no longer be about climate change, it will be about climate adaptation and crisis and emergency management. The ecosystem of business models will be reinvented. More frequent shortages of worldwide supply will prove that the perfect market macroeconomic theory of specialisation no longer holds true when the earth is in climate turmoil. We will see supply chain diversification and the return to regionalisation and even localisation of production within countries. We will see a short-to-medium contraction of investment returns as divestment in carbon and other things of the past occurs. We are the generation who will witness a wholesale transition from the shareholder economy to stakeholder capitalism. The worldwide transformation of business will happen at the global level and filter to economies everywhere. Who dares win but, in the end, it is a win for humanity.

Wherever change is happening, organisations must become better change makers. We need to help people in organisations to adapt. And that needs more, better, qualified change professionals to meet the demand. Is that you?

Chapter 1: Why be a Change Professional when you Grow Up?

To open this book, I told you the story of how I became a Change Manager in order to illustrate that many career paths can lead you to the role. There is no one set path. While that is what got me into change management, it is not what has kept me in it. What kept me in it is something else altogether. Let me tell you another story. In my early days at that first job as a Change Manager, to their credit, my organisation gave me time to learn more about what the role involved. The State's public sector had a project management framework in place at the time but it only had two paragraphs about change management. So, I went to my State Library and read every book on the subject I could get my hands on. Then, I built my first change framework from scratch. That experience was foundational as it gave me an intimate understanding of how change management works and doesn't work and where I could innovate in the future.

As I said, that's what got me into the role, but it's not what kept me in it for so long. One day, early into my first change job, a story came across my desk of a man who worked for a large well-known organisation in our country, who came to work one day and something had changed in the workplace. Tragically, he took his own life that day. That story hit me in the guts because, in my view, it was preventable. It was a change management issue. He had not been sufficiently informed or prepared for the change and the change impacted him deeply to the point of despair and disaster. At that time, I thought: "Not on my watch." In my role as a change professional, I still believe to this day, I can do something about situations like this. That story sparked in me a sense of mission to help organisations become excellent change-makers. Which means that they look after their people and aim to make things better. Or at least, to not make things worse.

That feeling of making a difference in even one person's life is what has kept me going for so long. What can change professionals do that make a difference? We can anticipate what a change is going to feel like for people. We investigate who is impacted and we 'see' them. My 'see' I mean the sense of actually seeing someone. There's a greeting in the Zulu language that I learned on a visit to Africa: *'sowabona'* (pronounced 's-ow-ah-bon-ah'), which translates as "I see you".

What we get to do in change management is a privilege. We get to be a respectful witness to people's pain as they go through change, we help them process it, work through it, get involved in it – if that's what they wish to do – and at the end of the day, we are with them as they celebrate their achievements of a change successfully completed. You'll notice I didn't say the change professional's achievement because it is never about us, it is always about the people we have the honour to serve. It's their change, their change journey and we are guides, who have one of the maps.

The change professional understands some of the territories on that map because we have spent time studying what people go through during times of change. We are experts on the theory of what can help. But each change is different. We get to study social groups to detect patterns of social interaction and influence and motivation and fears and values and psychological safety. We study the impact of past changes and what leadership means and even what the role of organisations is today and what people believe it to be and what that social contract means. There is a lot to it!

Then a change professional goes about constructing a strategy to help everyone move from Point A to Point B. People who I train to be excellent change people – which now includes you – will hear me often quoting a 'textbook definition' of what change management is. You've heard me say it already. I say it is "a planned set of activities designed to ensure that stakeholders utilise the outputs delivered so that business benefits can be realised". What you get to do in that remit as a change professional is exciting. I am a design-head by nature, I love interior design and garden design, and fashion design. In my view, change management is a design art. Except the canvas is the workplace and the subject of the art is the endlessly fascinating and constantly shifting topic of People.

There can be a lot of moving parts in strategising for a change and what I find fun is to analyse and work with people to come up with ways forward. We try things out and adapt to situations as they arise. No two days are the same in change management. I love the variety and I love the game. I find a deep satisfaction to see smiles on people's faces at the end of a change. All the while knowing that it all could have gone so badly and people's lives wrecked, all from the seemingly benign act of making a change in the workplace. That's why I would choose, again and again, to become a change professional when I grow up.

How about you? Are you ready to look within and find what skills you have that can be translated into the discipline of change management? Are you ready to step into change? Do me a favour, stop reading here, and make two lists for yourself. One is the skills that you believe you already have that could be applied to change. The other list is of the character traits you think a change professional may need to have. Later, once you are well into this book, you can compare your list to mine. Go do that now.

Chapter 2: Your Career Path Towards Change

You can step into change and craft your career in change management. Part of this transition is to put your current skills to work. Your first step is to know that it is expected that change professionals have at least one undergraduate degree. It's not impossible to get into change without it. But I find the practitioners who come with a well-rounded education, offered by a university degree, have greater abilities because university still teaches you *how to think*.

In terms of 'skills', that is *the ability to do something well*, there is a specific set of skills that can position you well for the role. Some common career paths that lead people to change management include: Organisational Development (OD); Training and Development, Communications, and Marketing. Also highly advantageous are: Project Management, Business Analysis and Risk Management. Any kind of degree in Business or Commerce is a really good foundation for change management. Of course, to transition to a new role, you need to start with where you are at.

This chapter is an overview of some of the common career paths to change management. It is a sweeping overview and each individual reader may have more or less skills and experience but it gives you a general picture. Below, find your current starting position and consider the perspectives of why we need you in change management and what you're learning edge might be, upon entering into your new change practice.

For Organisational Development folks: You already have people at the centre of your practice. You have a heart for developing others and helping them be the best they can be. We need you in change management because of your empathy. A further skill you will learn in change management is how to sequence and integrate change interventions into project management and business strategic planning cycles and how to project manage the people side of change. What you will find satisfying about change management is how well you can embed business strategy through double-purposed change interventions, meaning you advance a change while implementing business strategy. You already see OD interventions as being about progressing business strategy. The through-line for people from business strategy to the change is important. You will like the 'two birds with one stone' effect.

For Training and Development people: You are good at designing training strategies. It is a very similar skill to developing a change management strategy. We need you in change management because you will appreciate how training and capability-building fit in with a change management strategy, and you can organise an entire training program, if required. Sometimes, particularly on smaller changes, the training program falls into the remit of the change professional. If you have the widest possible definition of 'capability', you will see change management needs that others don't; such as gaps in change leadership capability, which can undermine a change. A further skill you will learn in change management is change analysis and the subtleties of understanding the current and future states for people and what that means for their training needs and acceptance of and adoption of the change. You could consider a specialisation of training and development within a change management practice.

For Communications people: You have command of the native language of your stakeholders. We need you in change management because, for our stakeholders, perception can be reality and you can guide them on a journey through words, stories and visuals. The ability to write well is so fundamental to change that all change professionals should be refreshing their communication skills often. Specialisms in science writing or arts writing can certainly be helpful in change because you can take a topic and bring it to life while being true to the technical content. A further skill you will learn in change management is how the communications strategy fits into the change strategy so that the entire set of planned activities support one another in holistic unison. You will learn that internal corporate communications is not change communications. But change management is not just communications. Change communications is an essential subset of change management.

For Marketing people: You know your stakeholders and you know how to influence them. We need you in change management because you align with the behavioural sciences by presenting marketing materials that take into account human motivation and what influences people. This can make a huge difference, not only to the outcomes of a change but to the targeted investment of time and energy along the way. By this I mean, in the implementation of change strategies, we do not have the time for scattergun approaches, often we need to get to the root of the issues and shift barriers quickly. Good targeted marketing materials can help, particularly with visuals. A further skill you will learn in change management is that not every change challenge has a marketing solution. You will learn how to layer tactic upon tactic in your stakeholder engagement plan from a wider range of influencing methods in your toolkit. I always say to my students that if you need to sell something, then something's gone wrong in your engagement plan. You will also learn about the seven different types of thinking modules, not just kinaesthetic, audio and visual (for learning beyond KAV, look up Dr Caroline Leaf's book 'Think, Learn, Succeed').

For Project Managers: You can schedule and sequence a lot of different activities to keep a change project moving. You have stakeholder management skills to engage the business to design business requirements and agree on the time, cost, and scope of a change. You have good discipline in the process of registering and managing risks, issues, and decisions, which is also needed in change management. We need you in change management because you understand how to make changes happen, through the vehicle of a project. That understanding of the project world means you know how to get things done. A further skill you will learn in change management is how to understand the people change risk, that is, the risk posed by the dependency your project has on people doing something differently in order for the change to be successful. A further skill is to understand what people experience as they go through times of change and what that means for the pace of change. You will learn how to truly step into someone else's shoes. You can also learn how to detect the underlying motivations of your stakeholders and understand why they act unexpectedly sometimes. One challenge you will have is being able to slice out just the people side of the change and go deep with it, rather than diverting your attention to the deliverables and schedule, and costs. The constant temptation will be to go back to what you know best, the PMing, but that will not progress your change management strategy enough. In many ways, you already do change management but – depending on the size of your project – have insufficient time to make it excellent.

For Business Analysts: You have advanced skills in working with the business to understand their business requirements. We need you in change management because you have the ability to comprehend the current and future state and what that means for business practice and change impacts. You have good skills in facilitation which is hugely valued in change management practice. The analysis aspects of change management and business analysis are almost identical. So many Business Analysts I have met, once they see what Change Managers do, say "Oh, we do the same thing!" Except the underlying drivers are subtly different, in that BA's define requirements and see impacts and Change Analysts analyse to find impacts so that they can design mitigations and interventions and then implement them. The cross-over of our work is in the change analysis aspect. Change professionals also do a lot of other activities. Good Business Analysts are highly underestimated. I love working with BA's, they have made my life as a Change Manager so much easier. For BA's who want to transition to a change professional role, your learning edge is to get your head around all the other change levers like change leadership, change communications, transition planning and even training and development.

For Risk Management folk: You have the discipline of risk down to a fine art. We need you in change management because you understand the interconnected nature of factors – strategic and operational – that can bring a change undone. Change management is a risk mitigation to business risk. A further skill you will learn in change management is how to implement risk mitigations in order to bring people's change risk down to acceptable levels and actively select interventions to harness the up-side of risk, business opportunities.

For Business or Commerce graduates: If you are newly graduated, then the world is your oyster and by the time you finish reading this book, I hope that you will consider change management as a viable and exciting career option. Although it might not feel like it at the time you graduate, you understand the language of business and drivers of business. We need you in change management because change is *for* business. Knowing how business works is critical to being able to manage change. Annual budgeting, strategy setting, rules around procurement, the language of contracts, how the micro-organisation fits into the macro economy, risk management, policies, and procedures – these are all the things that business is made of. A business degree teaches you a set of languages that you will speak in the workplace to make yourself understood and valued. A further skill you will learn in change management is putting it altogether from the perspective of your stakeholders and how to functionally and practically construct and implement a change management strategy.

What about other career paths?

There are many disciplines I have not mentioned and at the further risk of coming across as stereotyping, I have to point out that not all career paths lend themselves well to transition into change management. That said, if you recognise yourself in any of the job classes below but feel an affinity with the entry positions mentioned above, you may be in the wrong career in the first place. In my experience – and this is a huge generalisation – people who have come from engineering, accounting, law and science aren't as suited to change management roles as others. If this is you, it is OK to disagree.

- **Engineers:** While change professionals will be flexible in their approach and adapt to the mood of an organisation, Engineers will tend to see things more in black and white and want things to be logical, sequential, and understood. That's OK, I want my

Engineer to know exactly which part goes where so that what they are building for me lasts.

- **Accountants:** While change professionals recognise the shades of grey in people's espoused opinions and how can people can show up differently on different days, Accountants also are susceptible to perceiving the world as ordered, where everything has its' place in this column or that column. That's OK, I want my accountant to be precise to the cent and achieve balance. It's a play on words, I know, but change can be unexpected and unbalanced at times – and depending on the perspective from which you are observing a change – in reality, that balance once gone, sometimes never returns. Negotiating ambiguity is where change professionals thrive.
- **Lawyers:** I work with a lot of lawyers and have a lot of respect for their approach to life. While change professionals keep an open mind while hearing people out, lawyers will tend to want to argue from the first point made. That's OK, I want my Lawyer to have talent at arguing on my behalf.
- **Scientists:** People with a science background can go either way. The practice of experimentation with the physical world is not too dissimilar to the experimentation with humans in the social sciences. Change professionals have a high degree of interpersonal skills. When there are so many fascinating experiments to conduct in the lab, it just might not be a

scientist's thing to spend so much time with people, day in and day out.

Don't get me wrong, I love all these other roles. We need all sorts of diversity in the business world to make it all work. But they need change professionals working with them to shore up their natural tendency towards task over people. So they can play to their natural strengths and the change folk can play to theirs.

There are people in so many other careers out there and I do not have the time or space to address each one. There will be roles that I didn't cover. If that's you, then stay tuned, because we are about to cover what starter qualifications can shortcut you to step into change.

This chapter skimmed across many careers the world over and sectors simply to allow you to further reflect on you. What experiences and skills have you learned in your current or past workplaces that can be applied to change management? Go back to your list and make any additions.

Chapter 3: Have You Qualified?

This is a super quick chapter. My career vision is for organisations everywhere to be excellent change-makers. But there is a shortage of good change professionals. I wish more people would get qualified and join our profession, which is why I wrote this book. Workplaces are where a great many people on the planet spend the majority of their time. Change management can make a huge difference in people's experience of the workplace.

If you want to step into change, you need to know the qualifications that change folks must have. I've done my fair share of recruitment of change roles and this is my list of essentials. Remember, this is *after* you have a university degree.

The minimum standard: At the very minimum, the qualification that hirers look for is a Change Management Practitioner certification with APMG International. The training is based on the Effective Change Manager's Handbook, aligned with the Change Management Institute's Change Management Body of Knowledge (CMBoK). After completing this course, you can call yourself a change practitioner.

Hirers can look up an online register and find you listed amongst those who have completed the certification at https://apmg-international.com/successful-candidates.

The alternative minimum is a PROSCI certification.

Even after completing an undergraduate degree, having a certification is standard in the change guild. The change profession still only looks seriously at the folks who've done an accreditation like the APMG course or PROSCI. It is a rite of passage for change professionals.

Professional Memberships: Hirers will check that you have a membership to relevant professional associations. Join either the Change Management Institute or the Association of Change Management Professionals (ACMP), if you are American. Professional memberships show that you are serious about a career in change management.

Industry Accreditation: The APMG Change Management qualification gets you in the door. Then, eventually, you need to have industry accreditation. While the likes of an APMG course shows you know, an accreditation shows that you have actually done the job of a change professional. The APMG Change Management Practitioner certification takes 6 or so days to complete. So, anyone with funding can call themselves a Change

Manager within 5 days, after passing the exam. The barriers to entry are lower.

But with industry accreditation, the barriers to entry are higher, because it shows that you have real-life experience. It separates the sheep from the goats. An accreditation from the Change Management Institute as an Accredited Change Professional (ACP) is a real-world assessment designed to prove that you have the skills and experience of a change professional. The ACMP also has a Certified Change Management Professional (CCMP) accreditation.

Post-graduate studies: Several post-graduate courses in change strengthen your resume and knowledge. Finding a suitable course in your jurisdiction does take some planning. These include but are not limited to:

- Graduate Certificate in Change Management (e.g. from the Australian Graduate School of Management)
- Graduate Diploma in Change Management
- Masters in Change Management
- Master of Business Administration (Change Management)
- Graduate Certificate in Organisational Change
- Masters in Learning and Organisational Change

As a final note, qualifications in training and assessment are highly valued in change practice. There are many study options and some will be specific to your part of the world. Surprisingly, graduate study is not yet wholly essential to be a change professional. But it does tend to correlate with higher remuneration and all the other change professionals will often be reporting to them.

In this chapter, I listed the essentials for you to be seen as a qualified change professional in the employment market. Now, would be a good time to look up what qualifications are available in your areas or online. See which of the two professional associations is active in your region. Congratulations, by reading this book, you have started to craft your career in change management!

Chapter 4: Do You Naturally Have What It Takes?

Let's up the pace. We're going to fast forward to you looking for your first change job. If that last chapter on qualifications scared you, I'm about to reveal a little-known secret – a "career hack" – for a pathway to a change management job. Let's say by now you have submitted your application and you have made it through to interview for a Change Manager role.

Firstly, there's some bad news. It depends on who is recruiting you. I've often seen people in recruitment rounds who put their hat in the ring for a change job who have no qualifications whatsoever or who have not even taken webinars or seminars on change-related topics. Their pitch is that they have real-life experience of change happening to them and so naturally believe they know what it takes to be a change professional.

I get it, you have been through change and you hated it. You watched the leaders leading the change and had a thing or two to tell them about what people go through during times of change. They did it all wrong and you would do it oh-so-very-differently. Good change professionals can indeed be forged in the fire of soul-destroying change done badly. After all, that's where they learned lessons about what not to do. There are a lot of people "interested in change", but not interested enough to convert that to serious 5+ years of study and application as it takes to become a suitably qualified good change professional.

But recruiters like me – who know what they are looking for and are versed in change competencies – we want more to the story. Here's a test, when I asked you at the end of Chapter 1 to make two lists, did you? This is what I'm talking about. Let me challenge you, how did you get this far into this book, and you say that you want to work in change and then not take action and not take steps towards it? Please, tell me that you have done something while reading this book!

I'm not surprised that people put up their hand for change jobs when they have not done the prerequisites. In interviews, they come across as knowing what change is all about (career hack 1 – you too can do that). I've seen people literally quote from models they read about on the internet (career hack 2 – you too can do that). If you want that change job that badly, then hustle.

From my perspective, by the time you are in an interview, not having those qualifications and joining those professional bodies, shows that you were not serious about a change management career. So, the bad news is that you may not get through recruiters like me. From what I know now, I probably wouldn't have even recruited myself into my first role as a Change Manager. I guess I was fortunate because the role of Change Manager was rare in those days.

But – and listen up, this is an incredibly huge 'but' – there is a little-known secret window of opportunity to change roles. There's another side to the bad news. It's the good news: It depends on who is recruiting you. Wait, what! That sounds exactly like the bad news! That's because it is. Not all hiring managers know what they are looking for. It is so important that I'll say it again – it depends on who is recruiting you! Seriously. Some recruiters will hire you even if you do not have the qualifications or have had a past change job. They'll hire you on the simple basis that you have fire-in-the-belly passion based on experience of change done badly in the workplace and you sound like you know what you are talking about. Unbelievable but true.

If an organisation is recruiting their first change roles or their change maturity is very low, and you have shown enthusiasm for change, then you are still in with a chance. The reality is that a lot of organisations currently don't have the requisite discernment to differentiate one change management candidate from another. That situation may change in the future but today, it's reflective of what's happening. But, be aware, this hack is not surefire. You still have to go through the interview process and be selected on merit.

While this situation prevails, it means there are absolutely opportunities to land your first change job. Moreso if your selection panel does not have a change professional on it at all. You have the right to ask who is on an interview panel. No-one with "change" or similar in their title? You are in with a chance! If a professional recruitment company has not been involved, you are in the sweet spot. Recruitment companies are getting more savvy about change qualifications like APMG, competencies and accreditations like the Accredited Change Professional.

You can get a look-in by demonstrating an interest in change management.

- Career hack 1 is to take some webinar classes. Udemy is not a bad place to start. To get the interview in the first place, your CV had to look like a Change Manager's. List them in your CV. You can come across as knowing what change is all about. School the panel in the room.
- Career hack 2 is to look up a few change models and get to know the language. Look up John Kotter, ADKAR, and CMBOK. Pick up some books about change (as you have done with this one meaning you are ahead of many others already). Add Paul

Gibbons to your reading list for a contemporary evidence-based view.

While the employment markets are struggling to find people to fill all sorts of positions, opportunities exist for you. While recruiters of change roles are still unaware of what to look out for, opportunities exist for you. This is the loophole for those with no qualifications, nor experience but just keenness and some transferrable skills. But business is cyclical and these phases may end. Then that bow-wave will take with it the qualified, excellent change professionals towards the best change jobs that earn $200k+. Will that be you? Get to work!

Chapter 5: So, what about Change Leadership?

What if you've been a "Change Leader", can you transition to being a change professional? Many people worldwide aspire to leadership positions. Those who can lead change well have an enormous advantage in business. This is because they have skills in helping their teams to adapt. They anticipate how their people are going to react to change and have strategies and tactics already in place. But I've seen career managers step into a Change Manager role and not be successful at all. I observed a missing element – the hands-on approach combined with the discipline of some very specific types of planning that we use in change.

Change professionals are proactive and are involved both at the strategic as well as the grassroots level of a change. At the tactical level, there's a lot of what I call "grunt work" involved in change. Endless analysis of business impacts and a heap of reporting and operational change management processes, which need a high degree of organisational skill, specific focus and self-discipline. Not all managers are prepared to work like that. Some managers are mostly delegators. Delegation is also a change professional's toolkit, because we are very used to single-handedly recruiting change champions and all sorts of folk to help make the change successful.

But the managers who are hands-off and not proactive, do not make good Change Managers. I've seen organisations make that mistake, thinking that someone has led change so they can manage change. But that is not always the case.

There are competencies for leadership that do share similarities to change management competencies. But there are extra competencies for a change professional that are about influencing across organisations or across sectors. The Change Management Institute's Change Professional Competency Model details the deep skills like facilitating change, facilitation and co-design, coaching for change, and influencing others. These aren't your stock standard management or leadership competencies. They are specialist skills. I am not an advocate of teaching managers how to manage change, it is a different skill set to change leadership.

So much has been written about change leadership by John Kotter and other great business writers. There is a lot to be said for embedding change as a competency across all organisational roles. But it is a different set of competencies to that of a dedicated change professional. Often, we hear that change leadership is the critical success factor for successful change management, and that is still true today. PROSCI's annual research into *Best Practices in Change Management* consistently rates executive sponsorship as number one. With so much emphasis on change leadership in recent times, you would be forgiven for thinking that business theory is saying that change leaders need to *manage the change*. Strictly speaking, they don't.

John Kotter talks about the 'leadership coalition'. There is absolutely a need for a group of leaders to lead a change. It distributes the effort and shares the workload across a group. But who's coordinating the leadership coalition? Who's designing vision workshops? Who's clarifying what leadership actions each commits to, across the entire leadership coalition? It's not the organisational change leaders themselves, it's the change professional.

Individual change leaders don't have the bandwidth to manage the change. Often, they are leading multiple changes, which pulls them in all directions. Even a change sponsor may not understand the whole landscape at the depth of stakeholder analysis and change analysis that is required to be effective with change management. They need a change professional. A business manager has the remit to look after their own area and needs to rely on a coordination point for change management. There is a big difference between the role of leading the change and the actual coordination role, which is what we call change management. This is particularly true for larger transformation programs.

Be clear on that distinction. Change leadership is often confused with change management. This is because change leadership is the area of concentration – a "lever" – in change management. Change leadership is another sub-set of organisational change management. For all the emphasis on change leadership in business literature, one truth remains: change leaders don't have time to create change strategies. Change leaders cannot manage change. Change professionals do. Leaders do their change leadership role. They have conversations and talk about the vision, set the pace, govern the change, hold their staff to account, and much more. But the grunt work to put it all together into a cohesive change strategy and then, implement every little moving part takes specialist skills. You need a change professional.

All that said, what if you are a change leader right now, can you use your skills to become a change professional? Yes, you can, if you do what all other change professionals did to get to do the role – they get qualified, get accredited, and develop the character of a change professional.

Chapter 6: A Week in the Life of a Change Professional

Already we've covered the standard qualifications of a change professional. Soon we pick up a conversation about the type of character you need to develop in order to be successful. But first, I want to answer a question that I get asked a lot: what does it look like on a day-to-day basis to be a change professional? What people are really asking is: What do change professionals actually do? I'm assuming that since you picked up this book, you already have some idea of what change management involves. But for a quick overview, standard activities include:

- Analysis of the change – what will change, what is the future state, what is the vision;
- Analysis of stakeholders – who is impacted and how, what is their culture like and what will this change do to their world – physically and emotionally.
- Those data sets inform a change management strategy, which determines a set of designed tactics or interventions. The Change Manager develops and implements the strategy. Sounds simple, right?
- To illustrate to you, lovely reader, what I do practically on a day-to-day basis, I took a little notepad around with me for a week to

record it. With the title of "Director", I lead a Change Management Office (CMO) and a team of Organisational Change Leads. We have responsibility for an organisational-wide approach to change management in a public service agency of 1500 people. Here's a rundown of what I actually did that week:

- Monday – Even though it was a public holiday today, I chose to work 5 hours, a lot of the business managers like me in my organisation do. I drafted half a communications plan, populated names and groupings into a stakeholder analysis, drafted a PowerPoint version of a change management plan (because my client is visual) and I completed a facilitator's guide and associated PowerPoint presentation for a workshop on Friday. That workshop was my priority for the week.

- Tuesday – I opened my day with 90 minutes of focused work, as I do every day. I work well in the morning and my team knows that is when I do my best work. The work I do helps them do their work so they are fine with me not being available for the first 90 minutes of the day. They say it permits them to do the same. I focused on completing a facilitators' guide for a networking event I will be hosting on Friday for the State Service Organisational Change Management Community of Practice which I chair. The network has over 100 members, mostly located in the town where I live. We experienced a lot of growth in membership in the last year and I really wanted to spend this year helping people to connect and get to know each other a bit better. This was my second most important priority for the week. During the day I was at a lot of meetings including one-to-ones with my team members. We ran our team catch-up, where we talked about how last week went, what was on this week, any support we needed, and where we were working that week. It wasn't unusual for the team to be working across a few different sites on any one week – working from home, working at client sites, attending meetings in different offices around town. We have our business processes and ways of working set up so that we can work anywhere, anytime, and still be in touch with each other.

- Wednesday – I took a few phone calls today with potential candidates for a change role I was recruiting. Explaining the role to others gave me a new perspective on how far our Change Management Office had come in its first year of operations. One meeting in the morning was to review the change management plan for an IT system project the CMO was supporting. In the afternoon, we met with a business unit manager to debrief a change capacity workshop we delivered with their leadership team last week. The change capacity offering is a 2-hour workshop to map out all the changes a business unit would face in the next 12 to 24 months, which would impact their staff.

Once we have a map, we ask whether they have the capacity to deliver on all the changes. For other business units with which we have done that exercise, the CMO has then supported a range of change activities – people change risk assessments, the development of change plans, workshops on a range of topics, change capability training, communications plans and change coaching for managers and leaders. That afternoon I did a presentation at a local council about our Community of Practice, as we are extending our membership from the state government to local government.

- Thursday – I had a meeting to discuss the future state of a project. The change leaders developed a future state statement with additional associated operational elements to that which was described in the project plan. The discussion was around how the main change leaders were going to engage their reports about the operational changes and gain acceptance of new scope items. Then in the afternoon my team held its monthly mental health check-in meeting where we talked about our feelings, discussed any learning and development opportunities, and talked about any specific support we needed in the next month. In the evening, I had a board meeting with a global change management organisation.
- Friday – Today I facilitated a vision workshop for a business unit. The group was known to be disengaged and downhearted.

This workshop was the first step in an organisational culture change project I was co-designing. In the language of Human Synergistic Organisational Culture Inventory (OCI), their organisational culture was red, aggressive, and confrontational. The main protagonist was a highly technically skilled manager of whom the rest of the team was afraid. The week was capped off with a delightful networking session with our State Service Community of Practice. I felt like I got to know a lot of people in a way that I had not had the opportunity until then.

There you have it, a typical week as a change professional. At the end of each week, when I did my regular reflection, I felt again as though being a change professional was the best job in the world. In my role I get to interact with a variety of people: from senior executives to middle managers, from vendors and suppliers, from change champions to the people at the front line who are the end users of changes. I love the variety. With them I get to have interesting conversations about change, I get to make suggestions on ways to engage, I get to play with the design of engagements and activities, and I get to experiment and observe and understand the shape of a social network. It is stupendously fascinating work if you are interested in people. What I get to do and the people I get to work with inspire me daily.

Chapter 7: The Darker Sides of Change Management

Hopefully reading about a week-in-the-life sounded interesting, but as you are considering this career, you need to know about some of the darker sides of change management. Here, I'll walk you through a few of the big ones.

To get to the first scenario, I need to explain some background. I knew of it as the "agency effect" so I asked ChatGPT to tell me about it. After I said hi, (which I usually do because I like to treat everyone with respect including generative AIs. Also, just in case they turn on us one day). It said: Hey there! How's your day going? I prompted it so: "Great, I'm looking for a certain study. Do you know about it? It was about women going for a promotion and getting 14% less than men but if they were negotiating on behalf of someone else, they get a higher percentage."

It kindly reminded me: "There was a study conducted by Hannah Riley Bowles, an associate professor at Harvard Kennedy School. The study examined gender differences in negotiation outcomes and found that women who negotiate on behalf of others tend to achieve better results than when negotiating for themselves. Specifically, it found that women who negotiated for themselves received about

14% less than men, but when negotiating on behalf of others, they achieved comparable outcomes to men. This phenomenon is often referred to as the "negotiation backlash effect" or "agent effect." Hey, thanks ChatGPT, I almost had the term right. (By the way, full disclosure, this was the only use of ChatGPT I made in writing this book. Apart from helping me and some other humans such as OD practitioner, Susan Green, with the book title).

But the point is not about gender differences, it's about the Agent Effect I've seen in change professionals. They advocate on behalf of their stakeholders. Change professionals will go above and beyond for their stakeholders, whom they grow to care deeply about. The dark side of that agent effect is that this can unfortunately be a root cause for burnout. Another reason to appeal to you, dear reader, to step into change, because we need a pipeline of fresh new change professionals. The change professionals we have in the industry today are working very hard and, if they are not careful, they are going to burn out. Not that we want them to but it does go with the job. There are not too many change professionals I know who have not gone through at least one period of burnout in their career.

The second darker side is dealing with the fallout of redundancies. I have been lucky enough to not yet work on a change that resulted in people losing their jobs. Redeployment, yes. Reclassification, yes. The public service does not have redundancies as a general rule. But

I once worked in an organisation that implemented a lot of operational redundancies and the change was felt by the whole organisation. The change management was done by the HR department. In delivering the news, while the HR may say "It's not personal", it certainly feels 100% personal to the person hearing it.

The third darker side is dealing with cranky stakeholders impacted by a change. It is even worse when changes change. A change professional can be led to believe by a project manager that the change will deliver something specific or by a certain specific date. That has communicated with stakeholders, after approvals for change communications by the project manager or sponsor. But sometimes it turns out that the change needs to change. This could be caused by several factors. The quality of vendor deliverables turns out to be low and the project needs more time. Or the costs to deliver on requirements have risen over time and the scope of a project needs to be cut back to find value within limited budgets. A change professional builds relationships with their stakeholders and in these cases, you feel for your stakeholders' disappointment. But the dark side is that sometimes your stakeholders will shoot the messenger and their expression of disappointment can be aimed squarely at you. It can rock your sense of self and resilience to cop the thunder of cranky stakeholders.

To get to a fourth scenario, again, some background. In my experience, there are at least two different types of resistance. The first I call 'timely resistance'. Well-timed resistance is useful. I believe in the power of people collaborating. So much so that I composed a book about it: *'The Power of People Collaborating: Change Management Perspectives'*. Factoring in time in the change process to listen and understand, through genuine dialogue, is a key element to successful collaboration. There are opportunities at the divergent, early stages of a change for collaboration, cooperation, and for stakeholders to contribute to the final change design.

But there is another type of resistance, which I call 'untimely resistance'. And that can be expensive. This resistance occurs during the peak of an implementation. There will always come a time when no further additions can be made to the design of the change. It is a convergent time, where the definition of what is included in a change has been already made. An example is a building project, when the architectural designs are finished and the build is underway. Untimely resistance means costly delays.

I've seen something real that happens during a change, which I call the Ostrich Effect. A project will have put in a lot of effort to communicate what will change, to engage as many of the right people as possible and to identify all the right stakeholders but some key people may have passively resisted all along. Passive resistance is hard to spot. But then, right at the end of a change, just before implementation, the penny drops for that stakeholder and they realise the impact it is going to have on them and they finally speak up. They were at the table all along. But a firing amygdala can cause people to literally not hear what is being said. Suddenly the project repeats the same message for the 100th time and they're like: "Whoa, hold up, you are going to change *what*?" But the information they bring up at the 11th hour is legitimate and the change needs to change or it's just not going to work. That can be expensive! As a change professional, it is not your responsibility to feel people's feelings for them or do the act of listening and understanding for them.

Finally, on the darker side of change, ironically the mark of success for change is that not much happens! There is no fanfare at the lack of resistance towards a change and you were the one who swept the ice before it. There is no parade when a difficult stakeholder has adapted to the change and you know your actions, as the change professional, were pivotal in their turnaround. A change done well is smooth, business-as-usual, and often…well… a bit quiet. That is not good news for a change professional who need constant affirmation.

The character of a good change professional is that they are self-starters who can encourage themselves, without the need for thanks, recognition, or appreciation from others. It's a character of service to others. Like a little angel that dips in, makes a few well-placed adjustments and dips out again – job done. I find it nice when I get seen and recognised by those in the know but unless the managers around you know change management, they might not even realise that it was you. The best result you can hope for – and what you ultimately aim for – is that they think it was wholly them. I often use the quotation from the movie *Nanny McPhee* to describe how change professionals operate. She says: "When you need me but do not want me, I must stay. When you want me but do not need me, I must go." Since we've touched on it here, let's finally turn next our attention to the idea of the 'character' of a change professional.

Chapter 8: Do You Have the Character?

Already in this book, we have established a need in the world for more change professionals. We have investigated the different potential career paths that might lead you to change management and looked at day-to-day realities of the role. In this chapter, we build a picture of what a good change professional is. Before we do, I want to touch briefly on the concept of character. Why would we want to build a good character? I come from a Judeo-Christian worldview, in which I believe my role as a human is to transform my character to be more like Christ. Sure, there are business reasons to have good character. For one, it instils trust. But there is something deeper that has to do with my own transformation on this earth. From being a person who is self-centred to becoming other-centred. From being a person who is self-serving to becoming someone who serves others. From tearing others down to building up and encouraging. From taking to giving. In the daily work of change management, the ultimate point of it all is *who you are becoming*. Having a vision for the character you want to be is a starting point.

But don't be alarmed by that lofty aspiration; you don't have to have fully perfected your character before you go into the role. There is a wonderful phenomenon that happens when you do the job; the more you do change work, the more you improve your character. The nature of the job is such that you become a witness to other people's pain. For those who are actively self-aware, what that does to you at a character level is extraordinary and transformational.

One thing is for sure, your level of empathy goes through the roof. As you participate in people's change processes you realise that all the reactions you observe in others (sometimes in your face – vitriol, sarcasm, avoiding, aggression, cynicism, anger, and sadness; sometimes behind your back – avoidance, ignoring, complaining, and parodying) – all of those characteristics are *also within you*. The human experience has a kaleidoscope of emotions and the more I work with people, the more empathy I build. I cannot judge others for their reactions to change because, in their shoes, I would feel the same.

So, what does 'good' look like? I offer this description derived from an Adaptive Change Manager model, from the Change Management Institute. Good change professionals are all-rounders. They can think both strategically and tactically. They can hold conversations with ease at all levels, from the CEO to the cadets. They are highly competent and can adapt to different business situations and work with the leadership styles of different business managers. They are natural coaches, particularly in support of change leaders within the context of business changes.

They are project managers in their own right. They continually plan. Then implement. Then re-plan, then implement. Planning and implementation; in wheels of iteration, small and large. They have capability across the range of change management activities: change implementation, resistance management, change communication, change leadership, change strategy, change process, change success measures, organisational culture, change methods, models and frameworks, and reporting. If that's not enough, they also mobilise and nurture effective networks of change agents.

Good change professionals are adaptive and have a high level of curiosity about things and places and moreover, people. Their curiosity drives creativity, that ability to connect previously unconnected ideas, and create something new: new partnerships, new dialogue forums, and new connections between people. They have an innate instinct to ask good questions and they genuinely want to know the answers. They are good visual facilitators and can draw a change – literally with markers and a flipchart – to help people understand and relate. They use visuals as much, if not more, than words. But they are also digitally savvy and have a strong appetite for data – change data, business change impacts, and stakeholder data – and use data to align change plan activities, but they can also summarise data for executive audiences.

They practice 360-degree stakeholder engagement, meaning they look in every direction to survey and understand the stakeholder landscape. They go to the edges of a social system and encourage the outside to come in. They have a sixth sense when it comes to stakeholder sentiment and mood. They consider the linkages between stakeholders from one end of a business process to another. They are committed to diversity, equity and inclusion.

Good change professionals are sensitive to change fatigue and adapt the approach, pace, or volume of a change accordingly. They are highly self-aware, highly change resilient, and have advanced personal habits to manage their energy and focus their attention on deep work in order to maximise their productivity while enjoying rejuvenation periods to refresh and de-focus. Their character is of the highest standard, they don't gossip, they are discrete, and they call out behaviour that does not align with values. They have integrity. What is expected of a change professional is a lot to ask of any one person but it shows the breadth and depth that modern-day change practitioners need to have.

What about you? How did this list compare to the one you made at the end of Chapter 1? Do you already have some of the character traits of a change professional?

Chapter 9: Your Steps Towards Change

No matter what discipline you came from before moving into change or what stage you are at in your journey to get qualified, some transferrable principles from career transition methodologies also apply to change management. How do you get offered a change job without the experience? How do you get experience without being offered a change job? I already mentioned the loophole for those with no qualifications, nor experience but keenness and some transferrable skills. But that's not the ideal method and I would ultimately prefer you to get qualified and get some experience first. Don't be one of those who "are interested in change" but don't take action. It will not serve you in the long run. Your first step: get qualified (I know I'm hammering this point!).

Start where you are. My mother always said it is easier to get a job when you are in a job. If you are already in a job, to get experience, look around for opportunities to apply change management in the job you are already in. Even if you are in something like a procurement role but really see yourself in change, then put your hand up to create a simple one-page change plan so that everyone in your team can see what it is going to take to be successful. The process of figuring out how to do that will give you the foundation for your technical expertise and you can speak to it, as evidence-based STAR examples, when you start to go for change jobs. Besides, once you one day do your qualification, you will have that experience to draw on, which will make for a richer learning experience.

As an aside, if you don't know the STAR method of interviewing, it where you: state the Situation – for example, I was working on a tricky project with so and so organisation; the Tasks you had – I was given the responsibility to find a way through the trickiness; Actions you took – I worked with stakeholders to co-design the change management plan; and Results – the change worked well for such and such reasons and the organisation gained X% in productivity and everyone was pleased. Again, I'm still surprised at the number of people I interview who still don't have STAR in their basic toolkit. Don't let that be you.

Let me share a little real life story. The situation was: I once participated in an on-the-job business improvement capability program at work. It involved 150 hours of training followed by project managing a business improvement project. While change communication is a subset of change management, change management is a subset of business improvement. My Human Resources Director at the time said I could participate in the learning but not lead a project because I was needed elsewhere.

The training was excellent. When the other participants went off to apply what they learned, I created my own off-the-side-of-my-desk project, based on the Lean thinking methodology of "5S". 5S is a system that uses visual cues to reduce waste and optimise productivity by maintaining an orderly workplace and achieving more consistent operational results. I had access to an HR team and a heap of new knowledge. But it had to be small so as to not disrupt my daily work. Humbly, my action was to transform a shared storage cupboard to optimise its usage. The cupboard stored past training materials, facilitation guides, and textbooks for courses, handout booklets, some staff records, facilitation equipment, stationery, and more. It was shared by four or five sub-teams in HR and it was a bit of a mess and was almost unusable.

The result was that HR got a great new useful and optimised storage space. I also got the experience of leading a Lean project. But it was never about a cupboard, it was about applying my education, engaging with the HR staff about the concept, and bringing a group of interested people together to make an improvement. In case you didn't catch it, that was a STAR example. But in the same way, you too can find ways to do a change management project, exactly where you are. Find your cupboard.

Another pathway is to take a job working specifically on a change program, as a project officer or administrator or as a Change

Analyst. A Change Analyst role is an excellent grounding in learning how to handle those swathes of change data and to be someone who is great at using and even designing software solutions for change data and change reporting. Change analysis is an excellent foundation for more senior change roles. So, this tactic is to go for the entry-level change jobs and work your way up.

Another step on your pathway is to get some experience in a management consultancy which is doing change management work. Another surprising career hack is that organisations that engage management consultants don't always check if you are qualified in change management. Seriously, they don't check. They take it at face value from the reputation of the management consultancy alone and assume that surely, they've got people who are actually qualified in change.

There is always an option to go out on your own as a Change Consultant. If you are someone who is great at sales or if you have a great network, this could be a great option for you. Remember the standard activities you could offer as a Change Consultant are:

- Analysis of the change – what will change, what is the future state, what is the vision;

- Analysis of stakeholders – who is impacted and how, what is their culture like and what will this change do to their world – physically and emotionally.

Then, of course, those data sets inform a change management strategy, which determines a set of designed tactics. The Change Consultant develops the strategy for the organisation. The role is no different to a regular Change Manager. You can then negotiate a contract to implement it. Day rates as a Change Management Consultant are quite attractive but come at the expense of other benefits such as a regular pay packet and annual leave. It's a matter of personal preference in how you like to work and what's important to you.

We've come to our final career hack that will help you step into change and craft your career in change management. That is, to specialise in a sub-component of change management practice. This option can work really well with the change consultancy pathway because again, a lot of hirers of change consultants aren't really that clear on what a change professional does, so pitching work under the credible banner of a "change professional" can be fruitful. There is massive variation in the types of specialisations in change consulting available in the market.

The variation lies in the emphasis on different tactics. There can be specific distinctions between change professionals that place different service providers in different camps. You can be a change professional and also be a specialist in change leadership development work, be more training and competencies focused, or be more about change communications, or prioritise quality stakeholder engagement as your specialisation.

We even have change practitioners these days who mostly do behavioural economics and others who are solidly anchored in neuroscience. A lot of change practitioners use design thinking. Even Design Thinking specialists call themselves Change Makers. The practices used by change folk overlaps with other disciplines, which have all converged into an overarching practice called change management. These are all filters through which change-making can be done.

As it turns out, change professionals have as much variation between them as the different fish in tubs lined up in shaved ice at fish markets. The distinctions between different change management services make them confusing to compare, which opens up a whole world of opportunity for you, because business managers who are going to engage you, do not always know which type of fish they want to buy. If you pitch yourself as a "Change Manager", a lot of hirers will not yet necessarily know how to differentiate between you and the next specialised change professional. Not yet anyway, they're getting more educated and so this window of opportunity will one day close. So, get in now!

Chapter 10: Pre-decide your principles

As we're coming to the end of the book, I want to leave you with some final points to consider when the time comes and you have a bunch of job offers lined up. Of course, I want you to step into change. But just because you can get the work, doesn't mean you should take it. More specifically, I mean just because you can get the work with *particular organisations*, doesn't mean you should do it or should stay doing it. Once you are qualified and have some experience under your belt, then be choosy. Because you can. Change professional are in demand. Excellent change professionals are worth their weight in gold.

Firstly, truth be told, some organisations still don't understand change management. You might be the first Change Manager they have ever taken on. Expect that they don't know what you do, or what to do with you, or how to hold you to account and more importantly, assess your performance. In that scenario, you will find yourself doing a lot of education with your organisation about change management. I spent many years explaining the difference between change management, as in organisational change management – which is what I do – and technical change management, or 'change control', also known as ITIL change management. Just know that explaining goes with the territory.

Your approach will need to be one of patience and treating the introduction of change management as a project in and of itself.

While there is freedom in their ignorance, to run your own race and be highly autonomous, make great things happen; it can come back to bite you at performance time when you realise, they have not understood a word you have been saying all along. They think all you do is go out for coffee all day long with all those stakeholders and are unable to tell what difference you have made. When you were successful but your organisation does not rate it, then it's time to move on.

Secondly, like any recruitment process, you get to interview an organisation when considering their role. You must ask carefully crafted questions so that you can see the red flags before you bother to commit your time. How would they describe their culture? It is quite difficult to successfully implement change in highly toxic organisations. They don't need a change professional, they need an organisational surgeon! Unless the change gig is the culture itself, which might actually be an interesting ride for you but don't cut your teeth in an organisation like that.

Moreover, if you are a lone operator in a sea of toxins, it can be very challenging to make a difference. There are plenty of other organisations out there that have good leadership, are clear on where they are going, are employers of choice, are ethical, etc. B-Corp certified organisations are a great place to start. It's better to say no to an organisation where you believe you would never be able to win, than to become toxic yourself. Remember the burnout warning?

In an interview, ask the organisation how they know that change has been successful. Articulating success measures up front stops organisations from blaming you when the change goes south, when you, as the change professional, are not even accountable or responsible for making the actual change, the business is. Have your ears open to responses like: "Our managers hold the responsibility for the embedding phase of all of our changes and see it through until everything we need is in place." If you hear that, take the job!

In the interview ask how integrated their change management is with their project management. If it's a specific change you'll be working on, ask who is leading the change and what their role is. If it's a clear answer then that is hopeful. If the answer is: "Um…ah…hmm", not so much. But maybe that's the very challenge you are after.

Thirdly, the term "Change Manager" is encompassed by the term "Change Professional". The roles you may see advertised will vary. It might be called Change Specialist, or Change Lead, or Manager of

Culture and Change or Manager of Change and Communications. All these roles might actually do the same thing. But then again, they might not. Look closely at the role to see if it is really a change role, as per APMG or PROSCI. Sometimes if organisations are inexperienced with change, they will advertise for a Change Manager, thinking they are doing the right thing. It might be because someone told them they need to get better at managing change. But they don't really know what that means. I once applied for a Change Manager role that looked good on paper but by the time I got to interview, I realised they were really recruiting a line manager for an operations team. Why didn't they just call the role 'Operations Manager'? Because there were changes that they wanted to make. So, they figured it was a Change Manager they needed. It wasn't. Check the details of position descriptions and then ask questions of the hiring manager before you apply. If it doesn't have enough actual change work, then, you guessed it, say no.

Fourthly, especially say no to sociopathic and egotistical leadership teams. They cannot be helped because they don't want to be. The Nanny McPhee principle does not apply here. A change professional's life is all about service and if your key stakeholders don't want the service you offer for this reason, then don't offer it; say no.

Finally, say no to poor pay or working conditions, as it shows a lack of respect for your role. The remuneration must match the level of influence you need in the organisation. From the point of view of working conditions, if the role means you need to influence and support executives, then you need to have the organisational status to be able to do that effectively. From the point of view of remuneration, always negotiate on pay – always. Come at it with the agency effect – on whose behalf are you negotiating your remuneration? Your future stakeholders, your family, your community? If you are signing up for a fixed-term contract, then ask about the go-live date (or equivalent). If your contract ends the day after a go live, then say no. The embedding phase must be recognised as part of the change process.

Saying no to offers and having pre-decided boundaries about where you will offer your services will mean that your time and effort are leveraged to organisations and changes where you can have the greatest impact possible. That's what talent attraction is all about and you are the talent! The threshold for challenge is different for different people. The invitation here is to pre-decide the principles by which you will decide with whom to work. Here's one example of a set of principles:

- Principle 1 – I will not work for egotistical or dictatorial maniacs. I will work for and with leaders who are level-headed, humble and reasonable, leaders who listen and encourage and inspire their people to continue to learn and grow.

- Principle 2 – I will not work with completely broken-down organisational cultures where psychological safety is dangerously low. I will work with organisations which are ethical and sustainable and that operate with integrity and respect.
- Principle 3 – I will not work with organisations which do not respect the work that I do or my contribution. I will work with organisations who are willing to listen to the idea of experimenting with doing things differently. Organisations where people want to learn, work together and improve.

I encourage you to make your own list of principles before opportunities come your way. That way, you will have already decided how to discern one opportunity from another so that you can serve and make a difference.

Chapter 11: Put it Altogether

We've come to the end of our exploration of how you can step into change and craft your career in change management. Thank you for reading. What we explored in this book was:

1. Why anyone would want to be a change professional when they grow up.
2. Why there is a shortage of change professionals and where the future demand is going to be.
3. What essential qualifications and character traits change professionals need.
4. A week in the life of a change professional, with some practical insights into what the job involves on a day-to-day basis.
5. A warning about the darker side of change management, so that you can go into this career with eyes wide open.

We covered a lot of ground from qualifications, and accreditations through to character but at the end of the day everyone is individual and your path is your path. But I sincerely hope that one thing we share is an aspiration to serve our communities and organisations to become the best change makers they can possibly be.

Before we finish up, it's now up to you to keep the momentum going. Go back to those lists you made of the skills and character traits and let this be the basis for your next transition and learning plan. Find your cupboard. Get focused.

I hope this book has encouraged you to step into change. You are the next generation of change professionals. We need you!

Stay in touch! Connect with Naomi Jones-Black on LinkedIn and visit www.cmo-1.com/stepintochange

www.ingramcontent.com/pod-product-compliance
Lightning Source LLC
Chambersburg PA
CBHW071955210526
45479CB00003B/949